YOUR SENSATIONAL SENSE OF
TOUCH

BY JULIA VOGEL • ILLUSTRATED BY ROBERT SQUIER

Published by The Child's World®
1980 Lookout Drive • Mankato, MN 56003-1705
800-599-READ • www.childsworld.com

ACKNOWLEDGMENTS
The Child's World®: Mary Berendes, Publishing Director
The Design Lab: Design and production
Red Line Editorial: Editorial direction

LIBRARY OF CONGRESS CATALOGING-IN-PUBLICATION DATA
Vogel, Julia.
  Your sensational sense of touch / by Julia Vogel ;
illustrated by Robert Squier.
    p. cm.
Includes bibliographical references and index.
ISBN 978-1-60954-290-0 (library bound : alk. paper)
1. Touch—Juvenile literature. I. Squier, Robert, ill. II. Title.
QP451.V59 2011
612.8'8—dc22   2010037849

Printed in the United States of America
Mankato, MN
December, 2010
PA02068

ABOUT THE AUTHOR

Julia Vogel always feels happy when she's learning about science. An award-winning author, she has a bachelor's degree in biology and a doctorate in forestry. Julia's all-time favorite things to touch are horses' noses, crunchy fall leaves, and her children's hair.

ABOUT THE ILLUSTRATOR

Robert Squier has been drawing ever since he could hold a crayon. Today, instead of using crayons, he uses pencils, paint, and the computer. Robert lives in New Hampshire with his wife, Jessica, and a dog named "Q."

HI!

I'm Ice Cube. I love feeling icy! But I like how other things feel, too. Do you enjoy petting a kitten's soft fur? A friend's high five feels great when it smacks your hand.

Cold, soft, bumpy, bristly, sticky, wet. You can thank your sense of touch for letting you feel all kinds of things. But what is a sense? And how does touch work? Come along with me to explore your sense of touch. Let the tour begin!

BRR!

Wind stings your cheeks. The snow drifts down.

CRUNCH, CRUNCH, CRUNCH.

Your boots make deep footprints. Your senses let you know it's winter!

Touching, seeing, and hearing are senses. Smelling and tasting are, too. These five senses let you know what's happening around you. Cool, huh?

Your senses connect you to the world.

BRR! Cold lemonade cools you down on a hot day.

GROSS! Gum is sticky.

Roses smell good.
But they have sharp thorns.  **OUCH!**

Special body parts gather information about the world around you. Then they send it to the brain. Your eyes, nose, tongue, and ears are **sense organs**. But my favorite sense organ lets you feel cozy flannel sheets. It's your amazing skin!

Your skin does more than keep your insides in. It's also your biggest sense organ. But is every part of skin equally good at feeling?

Try this test. Blindfold a friend. Touch an orange to his leg. Then touch his leg with a fuzzy tennis ball. Can he feel the difference? What if he touches them with his hands?

The skin on your legs isn't very good at feeling things. The skin on your hands, feet, and face are much better.

Let's get under your skin. The top layer is thin. It is mostly flakes of old, dead skin. This isn't where you feel. Let's dive deeper!

Now we find a thicker layer. It is called the **dermis**. **Sensors** here gather information about the things you touch. Some sensors branch out like trees. Others coil like snakes around the bases of hairs.

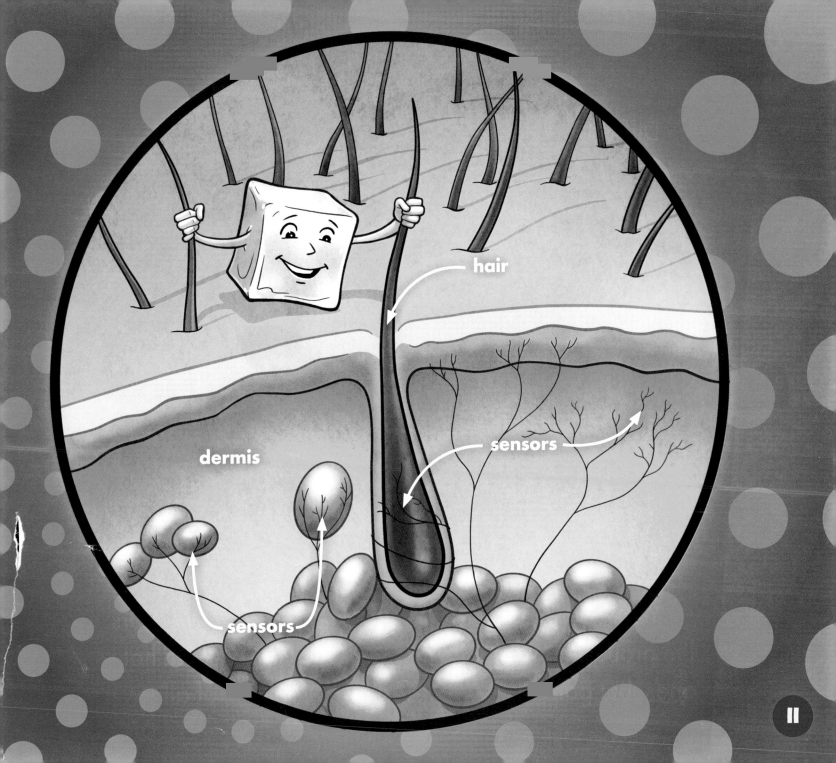

Different kinds of sensors tell you different things.

 Pain sensors alert you if you step on a sharp rock.

 **Pressure** sensors report that your big brother just sat on you.

 Heat sensors tell you a warm drink feels good after sledding.

 Some sensors feel hair movement. Brush that ant off your arm!

You have more of some kinds of sensors than others. I'm proud to say you have more cold sensors than hot ones. But pain sensors are the most common of all.

All of your touch sensors work together. They give you a whole "touch picture." An ice cube isn't just cold. It's also hard and shaped like a box. In your hand, a cube melts. Sensors tell you your hand is wet.

You can even feel an ice cube in one hand and warm toast in the other. That's because sensors are scattered all over your body. They can tell you different things at the same time.

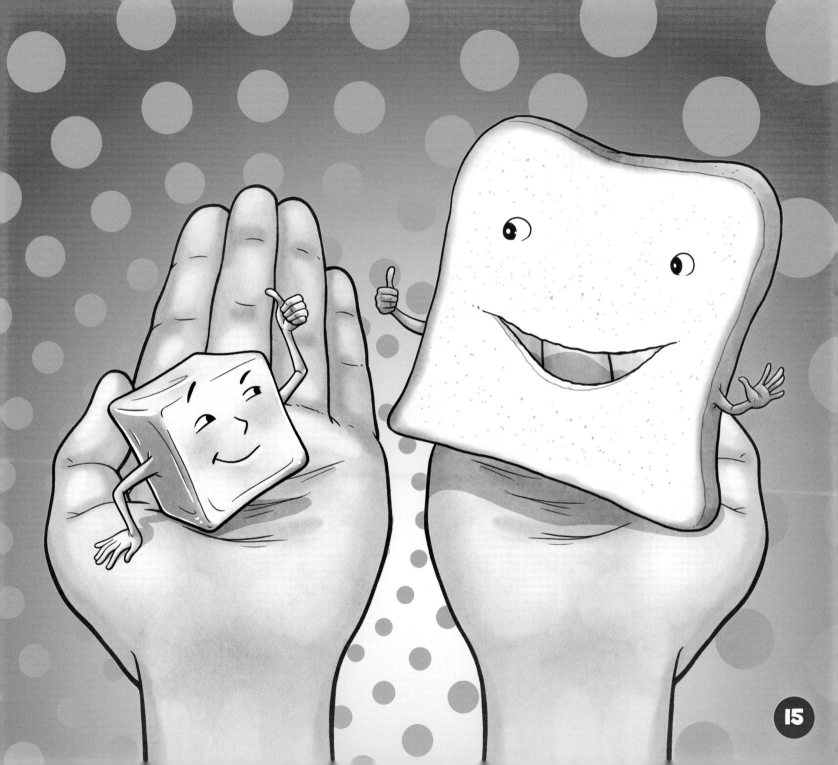

Your millions of sensors are constantly taking in information. How do you make sense of it all? The tour must leave your skin behind to find out.

The messages from your touch sensors travel away from your hand. They move very quickly along **nerves**. They go to your brain.

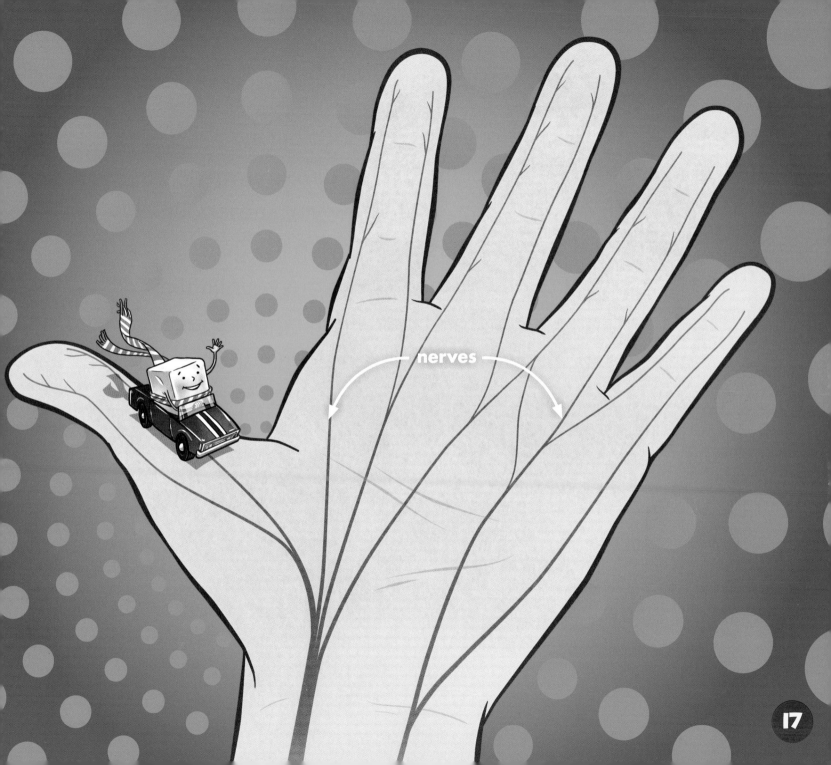

nerves

A special area of your brain sorts out the messages. This part of the brain figures out where the touch is happening. That's how you know your fingers, and not your toes, are playing the guitar.

Some extra-sensitive body parts are your fingers, lips, and tongue. They match up with bigger spaces in the brain. Your fingers have more brain space than your thighs.

touch center

brain

Next stop on our tour: your everyday life.
How is touch important to you? Touch can make
you happy.

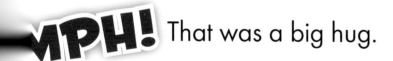 **OOOH.** That soft T-shirt is your favorite.

MPH! That was a big hug.

Touch can also mean danger. Pain can protect you
from getting hurt.

OH! A fire's heat says you're too close.

Sensors send touch messages to your brain day
and night.

Touch helps people **communicate**, or understand each other.

A handshake means, "Good to meet you."

A kiss on a skinned knee tells you, "I hope you feel better soon."

And a toe tickle says, "I like to make you laugh."

Some animals touch to communicate, too. When gorillas want to be friendly, they groom each other's fur. Remember that when Mom combs your hair.

Sometimes your sense of touch can go away for a while. It's never too cold for me. But on freezing days, your feet may start to tingle. They can even go **numb**, or lose their feeling. Stomp hard or rub them to warm them up.

A numb feeling can also come from medicine. A dentist may give you some before she fills a cavity. Your tongue feels weird! Normal feeling comes back when the medicine wears off.

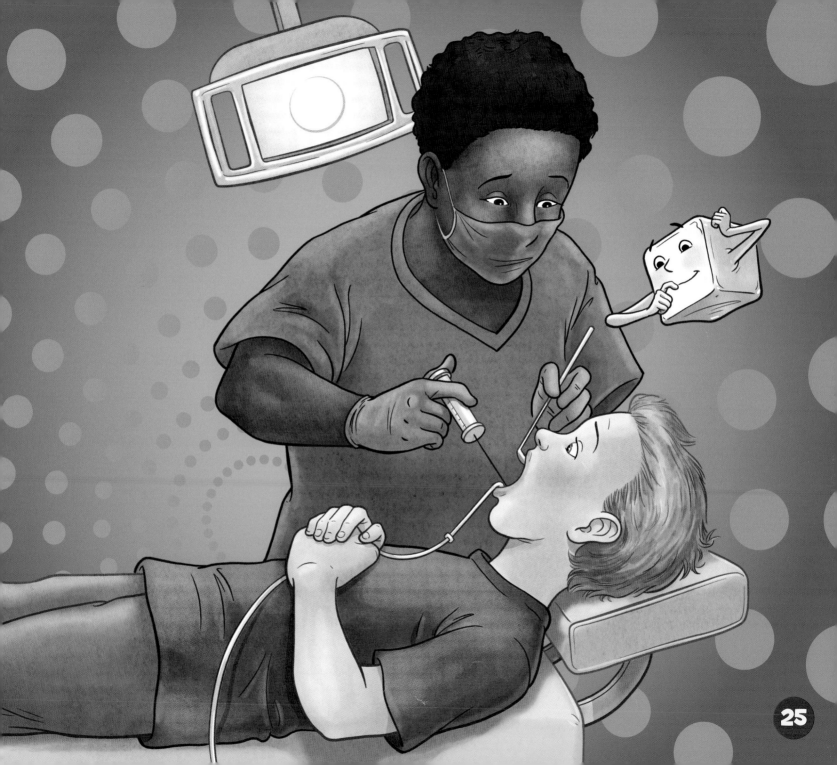

Sometimes people lose their sense of touch. Getting very sick or badly hurt can harm nerves that carry touch messages. **Diabetes** is a disease that can make people lose feeling in their feet.

But touch can also help people who have trouble with other senses. People who are blind may read using **Braille**. They make out words by moving their fingers along bumps on a page.

Outside in the wild, touch helps animals find food and avoid enemies.

I wish I could show you more about your sense of touch—like how it affects your muscles, bones, and other body parts.

For now, remember that touch helps you understand and enjoy the world. It's a truly sensational sense. Don't forget to stay in touch!

TOUCH TEST

Find out which body parts are most sensitive to touch.

Things you need:
bobby pin
cloth

Blindfold a friend with a cloth. Touch him or her on the fingertip with the pointed end of a bobby pin. Does your friend feel one point or two points? Try the test on different body parts: the palm of the hand, the back of the leg, and the elbow.

Switch places, so your friend is doing the test on you. At which places can you feel both points? What does that tell you about your touch sensors in those places?

GLOSSARY

Braille (BRAYL): Braille is a system of writing with raised bumps that can be read by touch. People who are blind use Braille to read.

communicate (kuh-MYOO-nuh-kayt): If people communicate, they share information, thoughts, ideas, or feelings with others. People can communicate by touch.

dermis (DUR-miss): The dermis is the second layer of skin. Touch sensors are in the dermis.

diabetes (dye-uh-BEE-tees): Diabetes is a disease caused by too much sugar in the blood. People with diabetes may not have feeling in their feet.

nerves (NURVS): Nerves are pathways that carry messages to or from the brain. Nerves carry messages about the things you touch.

numb (NUM): Something that is numb has lost its sense of touch for a little while. Very cold weather can make feet or hands numb.

pressure (PRESH-ur): Pressure is the feeling when something is pressed or squeezed. Some touch sensors in your skin sense pressure.

sense organs (SENSS OR-gins): Sense organs are body parts such as ears, eyes, nose, tongue, and skin that help you understand your world. Skin is one of your sense organs.

sensors (SEN-surs): Sensors are things that detect heat, pressure, or feeling. Some sensors in your body allow you to feel things.

FURTHER READING

Collins, Andrew. *See, Hear, Smell, Taste, and Touch: Using Your Five Senses.* Washington DC: National Geographic, 2006.

Landau, Elaine. *The Sense of Touch.* New York: Children's Press, 2009.

Walker, Richard. *Eyewitness Human Body.* New York: DK Publishing, 2009.

WEB SITES

Visit our Web site for links about your sensational sense of touch:

childsworld.com/links

Note to Parents, Teachers, and Librarians: We routinely verify our Web links to make sure they are safe and active sites. So encourage your readers to check them out!